# 50 Hearty Winter Dishes

By: Kelly Johnson

## Table of Contents

- Beef Stew with Root Vegetables
- Chicken Pot Pie
- Creamy Tomato Basil Soup
- Classic Shepherd's Pie
- Slow-Cooked Beef Brisket
- Baked Macaroni and Cheese
- Spaghetti Bolognese
- Chicken and Dumplings
- Beef and Ale Pie
- Mushroom Risotto
- French Onion Soup
- Lasagna with Garlic Bread
- Cozy Chili Con Carne
- Braised Short Ribs
- Smothered Pork Chops
- Stuffed Bell Peppers
- Slow-Cooker Lentil Soup
- Coq au Vin
- Vegetable and Bean Stew
- Beef Wellington
- Creamy Chicken and Rice Casserole
- Chicken Alfredo Pasta Bake
- Turkey and Sweet Potato Stew
- Jambalaya with Sausage and Shrimp
- Shepherd's Pie with Sweet Potato Topping
- Mushroom and Leek Pie
- Roast Chicken with Root Vegetables
- Cabbage and Sausage Stew
- Chicken and Chorizo Paella
- Slow-Cooked Pulled Pork
- Beef and Vegetable Casserole
- Butternut Squash and Sage Risotto
- Lamb Tagine with Couscous
- Chicken and Rice Soup
- Roasted Cauliflower and Cheddar Soup

- Classic Beef Stroganoff
- Potato and Leek Soup
- Slow-Cooker Beef Ragu
- Baked Ziti with Meatballs
- Chicken Cacciatore
- Beef and Sweet Potato Stew
- Spinach and Ricotta Stuffed Shells
- Vegetarian Chili with Quinoa
- Sausage and Potato Bake
- Braised Lamb Shanks with Mashed Potatoes
- Baked Sweet Potatoes with Sausage and Kale
- Squash and Bean Chili
- Fish and Chips
- Sweet and Sour Pork
- Stuffed Acorn Squash with Quinoa

## Beef Stew with Root Vegetables

**Ingredients:**

- 1 kg beef chuck, cut into cubes
- 3 carrots, chopped
- 2 parsnips, chopped
- 3 potatoes, diced
- 1 onion, chopped
- 3 garlic cloves, minced
- 1 cup beef broth
- 2 cups red wine
- 2 tbsp tomato paste
- 1 tsp thyme
- 1 tsp rosemary
- Salt and pepper to taste

**Instructions:**

1. Brown the beef cubes in a large pot, then set aside.
2. Sauté onions and garlic in the same pot until softened.
3. Stir in tomato paste, thyme, and rosemary, then return beef to the pot.
4. Add wine and broth, bring to a boil, and simmer for 2 hours.
5. Add root vegetables and cook for an additional 30 minutes until tender.
6. Season with salt and pepper, and serve warm.

## Chicken Pot Pie

**Ingredients:**

- 2 cups cooked chicken, shredded
- 2 cups mixed vegetables (carrots, peas, corn)
- 1 onion, chopped
- 3 tbsp butter
- 3 tbsp flour
- 1 1/2 cups chicken broth
- 1/2 cup milk
- 1 tsp thyme
- Salt and pepper to taste
- 1 sheet puff pastry or pie crust

**Instructions:**

1. Preheat the oven to 375°F (190°C).
2. Sauté onions in butter until softened, then stir in flour to create a roux.
3. Slowly add chicken broth and milk, whisking to avoid lumps.
4. Add chicken, vegetables, thyme, salt, and pepper. Simmer for 10 minutes.
5. Transfer mixture to a pie dish and top with pastry.
6. Bake for 25 minutes until the crust is golden brown and flaky.

**Creamy Tomato Basil Soup**

**Ingredients:**

- 6 tomatoes, chopped
- 1 onion, chopped
- 3 garlic cloves, minced
- 2 cups vegetable broth
- 1/2 cup cream
- 1/4 cup fresh basil, chopped
- 1 tbsp olive oil
- Salt and pepper to taste

**Instructions:**

1. Sauté onions and garlic in olive oil until softened.
2. Add chopped tomatoes and cook until they begin to break down.
3. Add vegetable broth and simmer for 15 minutes.
4. Blend the soup until smooth, then stir in cream and basil.
5. Season with salt and pepper and serve with a drizzle of cream.

**Classic Shepherd's Pie**

**Ingredients:**

- 500g ground lamb (or beef for cottage pie)
- 2 onions, chopped
- 2 carrots, diced
- 1 cup peas
- 2 tbsp tomato paste
- 1 cup beef broth
- 4 potatoes, peeled and mashed
- 1/4 cup butter
- 1/4 cup milk
- Salt and pepper to taste

**Instructions:**

1. Preheat the oven to 400°F (200°C).
2. Cook ground lamb with onions and carrots until browned.
3. Stir in tomato paste, broth, and peas, then simmer for 10 minutes.
4. In a separate pot, boil potatoes until tender, then mash with butter and milk.
5. Spread the meat mixture into a baking dish and top with mashed potatoes.
6. Bake for 20 minutes until the top is golden brown.

**Slow-Cooked Beef Brisket**

**Ingredients:**

- 1.5 kg beef brisket
- 2 onions, chopped
- 3 garlic cloves, minced
- 2 tbsp brown sugar
- 2 tbsp paprika
- 1 tbsp salt
- 1 tbsp pepper
- 1 cup beef broth
- 1 tbsp Worcestershire sauce

**Instructions:**

1. Rub brisket with brown sugar, paprika, salt, and pepper.
2. Place in a slow cooker with onions, garlic, broth, and Worcestershire sauce.
3. Cook on low for 8 hours until tender.
4. Slice the brisket and serve with the juices from the slow cooker.

## Baked Macaroni and Cheese

**Ingredients:**

- 300g elbow macaroni
- 2 cups shredded cheddar cheese
- 1 cup grated Parmesan cheese
- 2 cups milk
- 3 tbsp butter
- 3 tbsp flour
- 1 tsp mustard powder
- Salt and pepper to taste
- 1/2 cup breadcrumbs

**Instructions:**

1. Preheat the oven to 350°F (175°C).
2. Cook macaroni according to package instructions and set aside.
3. In a saucepan, melt butter and whisk in flour and mustard powder to create a roux.
4. Gradually add milk, stirring until thickened. Stir in cheeses until melted.
5. Combine pasta with cheese sauce and transfer to a baking dish.
6. Top with breadcrumbs and bake for 20 minutes until bubbly and golden.

## Spaghetti Bolognese

**Ingredients:**

- 500g ground beef
- 2 onions, chopped
- 2 garlic cloves, minced
- 1 carrot, chopped
- 1 celery stalk, chopped
- 2 cups tomato puree
- 1/4 cup red wine (optional)
- 1 tsp oregano
- Salt and pepper to taste
- 400g spaghetti

**Instructions:**

1. Brown ground beef in a pan, then set aside.
2. Sauté onions, garlic, carrot, and celery until softened.
3. Stir in tomato puree, red wine, oregano, and ground beef. Simmer for 30 minutes.
4. Cook spaghetti according to package instructions and toss with sauce.
5. Serve with grated Parmesan.

## Chicken and Dumplings

**Ingredients:**

- 2 chicken breasts, cooked and shredded
- 4 cups chicken broth
- 1 onion, chopped
- 2 carrots, sliced
- 2 celery stalks, chopped
- 2 cups flour
- 2 tsp baking powder
- 1/2 cup milk
- 1/4 cup butter
- Salt and pepper to taste

**Instructions:**

1. In a pot, simmer chicken, broth, onions, carrots, and celery for 15 minutes.
2. In a bowl, mix flour, baking powder, butter, and milk to form a dough.
3. Drop spoonfuls of dough into the simmering soup and cook for 10 minutes.
4. Stir in shredded chicken, season with salt and pepper, and serve.

**Beef and Ale Pie**

**Ingredients:**

- 500g beef stew meat, cubed
- 2 onions, chopped
- 1 cup ale
- 2 tbsp flour
- 1 tsp thyme
- 1 sheet puff pastry
- 1 egg, beaten
- Salt and pepper to taste

**Instructions:**

1. Brown beef and onions in a pan, then sprinkle with flour and cook for 2 minutes.
2. Stir in ale, thyme, and season with salt and pepper. Simmer for 1 hour.
3. Transfer mixture to a pie dish, cover with puff pastry, and trim the edges.
4. Brush with beaten egg and bake at 375°F (190°C) for 25 minutes until golden.

# Mushroom Risotto

**Ingredients:**

- 1 cup Arborio rice
- 2 cups vegetable broth
- 1 cup white wine
- 1/2 cup Parmesan cheese, grated
- 1 cup mushrooms, sliced (cremini or button)
- 1 small onion, chopped
- 2 garlic cloves, minced
- 2 tbsp butter
- 2 tbsp olive oil
- Salt and pepper to taste

**Instructions:**

1. In a large pan, sauté onions and garlic in olive oil until softened.
2. Add mushrooms and cook until tender, then remove from the pan and set aside.
3. In the same pan, melt butter and add Arborio rice. Stir for 1-2 minutes.
4. Gradually add wine, stirring constantly until absorbed.
5. Slowly add warm vegetable broth, one ladle at a time, stirring until each addition is absorbed before adding more.
6. Once the rice is tender and creamy (about 18-20 minutes), stir in cooked mushrooms and Parmesan cheese. Season with salt and pepper.

**French Onion Soup**

**Ingredients:**

- 4 large onions, thinly sliced
- 2 tbsp butter
- 1 tbsp olive oil
- 4 cups beef broth
- 1 cup white wine
- 2 sprigs thyme
- 1 bay leaf
- 1 French baguette, sliced
- 2 cups Gruyère cheese, grated
- Salt and pepper to taste

**Instructions:**

1. Heat butter and olive oil in a large pot over medium heat. Add onions and cook, stirring frequently, until caramelized, about 40 minutes.
2. Add wine and cook for 5 minutes until reduced.
3. Stir in beef broth, thyme, and bay leaf, and simmer for 20 minutes. Season with salt and pepper.
4. Meanwhile, toast baguette slices.
5. To serve, ladle soup into bowls, top with toasted bread, and sprinkle with Gruyère cheese. Broil for 3-4 minutes until cheese is melted and bubbly.

**Lasagna with Garlic Bread**

**Ingredients:**

For the Lasagna:

- 12 lasagna noodles
- 500g ground beef
- 2 cups ricotta cheese
- 2 cups shredded mozzarella cheese
- 1 cup grated Parmesan cheese
- 1 jar marinara sauce
- 1 onion, chopped
- 2 garlic cloves, minced
- 1 egg
- Salt and pepper to taste

For the Garlic Bread:

- 1 baguette or loaf of Italian bread
- 1/4 cup butter, softened
- 3 garlic cloves, minced
- 1/4 cup parsley, chopped

**Instructions:**

1. Preheat the oven to 375°F (190°C).
2. Cook the lasagna noodles according to package directions and drain.
3. In a pan, sauté onion and garlic until softened. Add ground beef and cook until browned. Stir in marinara sauce and simmer for 10 minutes.
4. In a bowl, combine ricotta cheese, egg, and 1 cup mozzarella. Season with salt and pepper.
5. In a baking dish, layer cooked noodles, meat sauce, ricotta mixture, and mozzarella cheese. Repeat layers and top with Parmesan cheese.
6. Cover with foil and bake for 30 minutes. Remove foil and bake for an additional 15 minutes until bubbly.
7. For the garlic bread, spread butter, garlic, and parsley on sliced bread and bake at 350°F (175°C) for 10-15 minutes until golden.

## Cozy Chili Con Carne

**Ingredients:**

- 500g ground beef
- 1 onion, chopped
- 2 garlic cloves, minced
- 2 cans kidney beans, drained and rinsed
- 1 can diced tomatoes
- 1 tbsp chili powder
- 1 tsp cumin
- 1 tsp paprika
- 1/2 tsp cayenne pepper (optional)
- 2 cups beef broth
- Salt and pepper to taste
- Toppings: sour cream, shredded cheese, green onions

**Instructions:**

1. In a large pot, sauté onions and garlic until softened. Add ground beef and cook until browned.
2. Stir in chili powder, cumin, paprika, and cayenne. Cook for 1 minute.
3. Add beans, tomatoes, beef broth, and season with salt and pepper. Bring to a simmer and cook for 45 minutes.
4. Serve with your favorite toppings like sour cream, cheese, and green onions.

# Braised Short Ribs

**Ingredients:**

- 1.5 kg beef short ribs
- 2 tbsp olive oil
- 2 onions, chopped
- 2 carrots, chopped
- 2 celery stalks, chopped
- 2 garlic cloves, minced
- 2 cups red wine
- 4 cups beef broth
- 1 sprig thyme
- 1 bay leaf
- Salt and pepper to taste

**Instructions:**

1. Preheat oven to 350°F (175°C).
2. Heat olive oil in a large ovenproof pot. Brown short ribs on all sides, then remove and set aside.
3. In the same pot, sauté onions, carrots, celery, and garlic until softened.
4. Pour in wine and scrape the bottom to deglaze the pot. Add beef broth, thyme, and bay leaf.
5. Return short ribs to the pot, cover, and bake for 2.5-3 hours until the meat is tender.
6. Serve with mashed potatoes or crusty bread.

## Smothered Pork Chops

**Ingredients:**

- 4 bone-in pork chops
- 1 onion, sliced
- 2 garlic cloves, minced
- 2 cups chicken broth
- 1 tbsp flour
- 1 tbsp olive oil
- 1 tsp thyme
- Salt and pepper to taste

**Instructions:**

1. Heat olive oil in a pan and brown pork chops on both sides. Remove and set aside.
2. In the same pan, sauté onions and garlic until softened. Stir in flour to make a roux.
3. Gradually add chicken broth, whisking until smooth. Add thyme and season with salt and pepper.
4. Return pork chops to the pan and simmer for 30 minutes, covering to let the sauce thicken.
5. Serve with mashed potatoes or rice.

## Stuffed Bell Peppers

**Ingredients:**

- 4 bell peppers, tops cut off and seeds removed
- 500g ground beef
- 1 cup cooked rice
- 1 onion, chopped
- 2 garlic cloves, minced
- 1 can diced tomatoes
- 1 tsp oregano
- 1/2 cup shredded mozzarella cheese
- Salt and pepper to taste

**Instructions:**

1. Preheat oven to 375°F (190°C).
2. Cook ground beef, onion, and garlic in a pan until browned. Stir in rice, tomatoes, oregano, salt, and pepper.
3. Stuff the peppers with the beef mixture and place in a baking dish.
4. Top with shredded mozzarella and bake for 25 minutes until peppers are tender.

**Slow-Cooker Lentil Soup**

**Ingredients:**

- 2 cups dried lentils
- 1 onion, chopped
- 2 carrots, diced
- 2 celery stalks, chopped
- 3 garlic cloves, minced
- 4 cups vegetable broth
- 1 can diced tomatoes
- 1 tsp cumin
- Salt and pepper to taste

**Instructions:**

1. In a slow cooker, combine lentils, onions, carrots, celery, garlic, broth, tomatoes, cumin, salt, and pepper.
2. Cook on low for 6-8 hours until lentils are tender.
3. Serve with crusty bread.

**Coq au Vin**

**Ingredients:**

- 1 whole chicken, cut into pieces
- 2 cups red wine (Burgundy preferred)
- 2 cups chicken broth
- 2 onions, chopped
- 2 carrots, chopped
- 2 garlic cloves, minced
- 2 sprigs thyme
- 1 bay leaf
- 150g mushrooms, sliced
- 150g bacon, diced
- Salt and pepper to taste

**Instructions:**

1. Brown chicken pieces in a large pot with bacon, then remove and set aside.
2. Sauté onions, carrots, and garlic until softened. Add mushrooms and cook for 5 minutes.
3. Add wine and chicken broth, then return chicken to the pot with thyme, bay leaf, salt, and pepper.
4. Cover and simmer for 1.5 hours until chicken is tender.
5. Serve with mashed potatoes or baguette.

## Vegetable and Bean Stew

**Ingredients:**

- 1 tbsp olive oil
- 1 onion, chopped
- 2 garlic cloves, minced
- 2 carrots, diced
- 2 celery stalks, chopped
- 1 zucchini, chopped
- 1 can cannellini beans, drained and rinsed
- 1 can diced tomatoes
- 4 cups vegetable broth
- 1 tsp thyme
- 1 tsp rosemary
- Salt and pepper to taste
- 1 cup spinach or kale

**Instructions:**

1. Heat olive oil in a large pot over medium heat. Add onion and garlic, cooking until softened.
2. Add carrots, celery, zucchini, and cook for 5 minutes.
3. Stir in beans, tomatoes, vegetable broth, thyme, rosemary, salt, and pepper. Bring to a boil, then reduce to a simmer for 30 minutes.
4. Stir in spinach or kale and cook for another 5 minutes.
5. Serve with crusty bread.

## Beef Wellington

**Ingredients:**

- 1 kg beef tenderloin, trimmed
- 2 tbsp olive oil
- 200g mushrooms, finely chopped
- 2 tbsp Dijon mustard
- 1 sheet puff pastry
- 1 egg, beaten
- 1/2 cup prosciutto slices
- Salt and pepper to taste

**Instructions:**

1. Preheat oven to 400°F (200°C).
2. Heat olive oil in a pan, season beef with salt and pepper, then sear on all sides until browned. Brush with Dijon mustard and set aside to cool.
3. In the same pan, sauté mushrooms until moisture evaporates, then let cool.
4. Lay prosciutto on a sheet of plastic wrap, spread mushrooms over it, and roll the beef in the mixture.
5. Unroll the puff pastry and wrap the beef inside. Seal the edges and brush with beaten egg.
6. Bake for 25-30 minutes or until pastry is golden and beef is medium-rare.
7. Let rest for 10 minutes before slicing and serving.

**Creamy Chicken and Rice Casserole**

**Ingredients:**

- 2 cups cooked chicken, shredded
- 1 cup cooked rice
- 1 can cream of chicken soup
- 1/2 cup sour cream
- 1/2 cup shredded cheddar cheese
- 1 small onion, chopped
- 1 garlic clove, minced
- 1 cup frozen peas
- Salt and pepper to taste
- 1/2 cup breadcrumbs

**Instructions:**

1. Preheat oven to 350°F (175°C).
2. In a large bowl, combine chicken, rice, cream of chicken soup, sour cream, cheddar cheese, onion, garlic, peas, salt, and pepper.
3. Transfer to a greased baking dish and top with breadcrumbs.
4. Bake for 25-30 minutes until bubbly and golden on top.
5. Serve warm.

## Chicken Alfredo Pasta Bake

**Ingredients:**

- 3 cups cooked chicken, shredded
- 12 oz pasta (penne or rigatoni)
- 2 cups heavy cream
- 1 cup grated Parmesan cheese
- 1 cup shredded mozzarella cheese
- 2 garlic cloves, minced
- 2 tbsp butter
- Salt and pepper to taste
- 1 tbsp parsley, chopped

**Instructions:**

1. Preheat oven to 375°F (190°C).
2. Cook pasta according to package directions, then drain.
3. In a pan, melt butter and sauté garlic for 1 minute. Add heavy cream, Parmesan, salt, and pepper. Stir and cook for 5 minutes.
4. Combine pasta, chicken, and sauce in a baking dish. Top with mozzarella cheese and bake for 20-25 minutes.
5. Garnish with parsley and serve hot.

**Turkey and Sweet Potato Stew**

**Ingredients:**

- 1 lb turkey breast, cubed
- 2 tbsp olive oil
- 1 onion, chopped
- 2 garlic cloves, minced
- 2 sweet potatoes, peeled and cubed
- 1 can diced tomatoes
- 4 cups chicken broth
- 1 tsp thyme
- 1 tsp cumin
- Salt and pepper to taste
- 2 cups spinach or kale

**Instructions:**

1. Heat olive oil in a large pot. Add turkey and cook until browned. Remove and set aside.
2. In the same pot, sauté onions and garlic until softened.
3. Add sweet potatoes, tomatoes, chicken broth, thyme, cumin, salt, and pepper. Bring to a boil, then simmer for 25 minutes.
4. Stir in spinach or kale and cook for another 5 minutes.
5. Serve hot with crusty bread.

# Jambalaya with Sausage and Shrimp

**Ingredients:**

- 1 tbsp olive oil
- 1 onion, chopped
- 1 bell pepper, chopped
- 2 garlic cloves, minced
- 1 lb sausage, sliced
- 1 lb shrimp, peeled and deveined
- 2 cups rice
- 1 can diced tomatoes
- 4 cups chicken broth
- 1 tsp paprika
- 1 tsp thyme
- 1 bay leaf
- Salt and pepper to taste

**Instructions:**

1. Heat olive oil in a large pot. Add sausage and cook until browned, then set aside.
2. Sauté onion, bell pepper, and garlic until softened.
3. Stir in rice, diced tomatoes, chicken broth, paprika, thyme, bay leaf, and season with salt and pepper.
4. Bring to a boil, then reduce to a simmer for 20 minutes.
5. Add shrimp and cooked sausage, then simmer for an additional 5-7 minutes until shrimp are cooked through.
6. Serve warm.

## Shepherd's Pie with Sweet Potato Topping

**Ingredients:**

- 1 lb ground lamb or beef
- 1 onion, chopped
- 2 carrots, diced
- 1 cup peas
- 1 cup beef broth
- 2 tbsp tomato paste
- 1 tsp thyme
- Salt and pepper to taste
- 4 sweet potatoes, peeled and cubed
- 2 tbsp butter
- 1/4 cup milk

**Instructions:**

1. Preheat oven to 375°F (190°C).
2. Cook the ground meat in a pan, then add onions, carrots, and peas. Stir in tomato paste, beef broth, thyme, salt, and pepper. Simmer for 10 minutes.
3. Meanwhile, cook sweet potatoes in boiling water until tender. Mash with butter and milk.
4. Spread the meat mixture in a baking dish and top with mashed sweet potatoes.
5. Bake for 20 minutes until the top is golden.
6. Serve warm.

## Mushroom and Leek Pie

**Ingredients:**

- 2 tbsp olive oil
- 2 leeks, sliced
- 2 cups mushrooms, chopped
- 1/2 cup vegetable broth
- 1/2 cup heavy cream
- 1 sheet puff pastry
- Salt and pepper to taste

**Instructions:**

1. Preheat oven to 375°F (190°C).
2. Heat olive oil in a pan, then sauté leeks and mushrooms until softened.
3. Add broth and cream, simmer until thickened. Season with salt and pepper.
4. Transfer mixture to a pie dish, then cover with puff pastry. Seal edges and bake for 25-30 minutes.
5. Serve hot.

**Roast Chicken with Root Vegetables**

**Ingredients:**

- 1 whole chicken (3-4 lbs)
- 4 carrots, chopped
- 4 potatoes, chopped
- 1 onion, quartered
- 4 garlic cloves, smashed
- 2 tbsp olive oil
- 1 tbsp rosemary, chopped
- Salt and pepper to taste

**Instructions:**

1. Preheat oven to 425°F (220°C).
2. Place chicken on a roasting pan, rub with olive oil, and season with salt, pepper, and rosemary.
3. Arrange carrots, potatoes, onions, and garlic around the chicken.
4. Roast for 1-1.5 hours until chicken is golden and juices run clear.
5. Let rest for 10 minutes before serving with vegetables.

**Cabbage and Sausage Stew**

**Ingredients:**

- 1 lb sausage, sliced
- 1 onion, chopped
- 2 garlic cloves, minced
- 4 cups cabbage, shredded
- 4 potatoes, diced
- 4 cups chicken broth
- 1 tsp thyme
- Salt and pepper to taste

**Instructions:**

1. Heat a large pot over medium heat and brown the sausage. Remove and set aside.
2. In the same pot, sauté onion and garlic until softened.
3. Add cabbage, potatoes, chicken broth, thyme, salt, and pepper. Bring to a boil, then reduce to a simmer for 30 minutes.
4. Add sausage back in and cook for an additional 10 minutes.
5. Serve hot with crusty bread.

**Chicken and Chorizo Paella**

**Ingredients:**

- 1 lb chicken thighs, diced
- 1/2 lb chorizo, sliced
- 1 onion, chopped
- 2 garlic cloves, minced
- 1 red bell pepper, chopped
- 1 cup Arborio rice
- 1 can diced tomatoes
- 2 cups chicken broth
- 1/2 tsp saffron threads
- 1/2 tsp paprika
- Salt and pepper to taste
- 1/2 cup peas
- 1 tbsp parsley, chopped

**Instructions:**

1. Heat olive oil in a large pan over medium heat. Brown chicken and chorizo, then remove from the pan.
2. Sauté onion, garlic, and bell pepper until softened.
3. Stir in rice, diced tomatoes, chicken broth, saffron, paprika, salt, and pepper. Bring to a boil.
4. Reduce heat and simmer for 20-25 minutes until rice is tender and liquid is absorbed.
5. Add peas, return chicken and chorizo to the pan, and cook for another 5 minutes.
6. Garnish with parsley and serve.

## Slow-Cooked Pulled Pork

**Ingredients:**

- 3 lb pork shoulder
- 1 onion, chopped
- 4 garlic cloves, minced
- 1/4 cup apple cider vinegar
- 1/4 cup BBQ sauce
- 1 tsp smoked paprika
- 1/2 tsp cumin
- Salt and pepper to taste

**Instructions:**

1. Place the pork shoulder in a slow cooker and rub with smoked paprika, cumin, salt, and pepper.
2. Add onion, garlic, apple cider vinegar, and BBQ sauce to the slow cooker.
3. Cook on low for 8-10 hours until the pork is tender and easily shredded.
4. Shred the pork with a fork and serve with extra BBQ sauce on buns or with sides of your choice.

**Beef and Vegetable Casserole**

**Ingredients:**

- 1 lb beef stew meat
- 2 tbsp olive oil
- 2 onions, chopped
- 3 carrots, sliced
- 2 potatoes, diced
- 1 cup peas
- 4 cups beef broth
- 1 tsp thyme
- Salt and pepper to taste
- 1/4 cup flour

**Instructions:**

1. Heat olive oil in a large pot over medium heat. Brown the beef stew meat in batches, then set aside.
2. In the same pot, sauté onions, carrots, and potatoes until softened.
3. Add the beef back in, then sprinkle with flour. Stir to coat and cook for 2 minutes.
4. Pour in beef broth, thyme, salt, and pepper. Bring to a boil, then reduce to a simmer for 1-1.5 hours until the beef is tender.
5. Stir in peas and cook for another 10 minutes.
6. Serve warm with crusty bread.

## Butternut Squash and Sage Risotto

**Ingredients:**

- 1 tbsp olive oil
- 1 small butternut squash, peeled and cubed
- 1 onion, chopped
- 2 garlic cloves, minced
- 1 cup Arborio rice
- 4 cups vegetable broth
- 1/2 cup white wine
- 1/2 cup Parmesan cheese
- 1 tbsp fresh sage, chopped
- Salt and pepper to taste

**Instructions:**

1. Preheat oven to 400°F (200°C). Toss squash with olive oil, salt, and pepper, then roast for 25-30 minutes until tender.
2. In a pan, sauté onion and garlic in olive oil until softened. Add rice and cook for 2 minutes.
3. Pour in white wine and stir until absorbed.
4. Add broth, one cup at a time, stirring constantly and letting it absorb before adding more.
5. Once the rice is creamy and tender, stir in roasted squash, Parmesan, and sage.
6. Season with salt and pepper and serve hot.

**Lamb Tagine with Couscous**

**Ingredients:**

- 2 lbs lamb, cubed
- 1 tbsp olive oil
- 1 onion, chopped
- 2 garlic cloves, minced
- 1 tsp cumin
- 1 tsp cinnamon
- 1/2 tsp turmeric
- 1/2 tsp paprika
- 1 can diced tomatoes
- 1 cup vegetable broth
- 1/2 cup raisins
- 1 tbsp honey
- Salt and pepper to taste
- 1 1/2 cups couscous

**Instructions:**

1. Heat olive oil in a large pot over medium heat. Brown the lamb in batches, then set aside.
2. Sauté onion and garlic until softened. Add spices and cook for 1 minute.
3. Stir in diced tomatoes, vegetable broth, raisins, honey, salt, and pepper. Bring to a simmer.
4. Return lamb to the pot, cover, and cook for 1.5-2 hours until tender.
5. Cook couscous according to package instructions, fluff with a fork.
6. Serve lamb tagine over couscous.

**Chicken and Rice Soup**

**Ingredients:**

- 2 tbsp olive oil
- 1 onion, chopped
- 2 carrots, diced
- 2 celery stalks, chopped
- 2 garlic cloves, minced
- 1 cup cooked chicken, shredded
- 1 cup rice
- 6 cups chicken broth
- 1 tsp thyme
- Salt and pepper to taste

**Instructions:**

1. Heat olive oil in a large pot. Sauté onion, carrots, celery, and garlic until softened.
2. Stir in chicken, rice, chicken broth, thyme, salt, and pepper. Bring to a boil.
3. Reduce heat and simmer for 20-25 minutes until rice is cooked and tender.
4. Serve hot with crusty bread.

## Roasted Cauliflower and Cheddar Soup

**Ingredients:**

- 1 head cauliflower, chopped
- 2 tbsp olive oil
- 1 onion, chopped
- 2 garlic cloves, minced
- 4 cups vegetable broth
- 1/2 cup cheddar cheese, shredded
- Salt and pepper to taste

**Instructions:**

1. Preheat oven to 425°F (220°C). Toss cauliflower with olive oil, salt, and pepper, then roast for 25-30 minutes until tender.
2. In a pot, sauté onion and garlic until softened. Add roasted cauliflower and vegetable broth.
3. Bring to a boil, then simmer for 10 minutes. Use an immersion blender to blend the soup until smooth.
4. Stir in cheddar cheese and cook until melted.
5. Serve warm with extra cheese on top.

## Classic Beef Stroganoff

**Ingredients:**

- 1 lb beef tenderloin, thinly sliced
- 1 tbsp olive oil
- 1 onion, chopped
- 2 garlic cloves, minced
- 1 cup mushrooms, sliced
- 1/2 cup sour cream
- 1/2 cup beef broth
- 1 tbsp Worcestershire sauce
- Salt and pepper to taste
- 2 tbsp flour

**Instructions:**

1. Heat olive oil in a pan and cook beef until browned, then remove and set aside.
2. Sauté onion, garlic, and mushrooms until softened.
3. Stir in flour and cook for 2 minutes. Add beef broth, Worcestershire sauce, and salt and pepper.
4. Return beef to the pan and simmer for 5 minutes. Stir in sour cream and cook for another 2 minutes.
5. Serve over egg noodles or rice.

## Potato and Leek Soup

**Ingredients:**

- 4 large potatoes, peeled and diced
- 3 leeks, cleaned and chopped
- 2 tbsp olive oil
- 1 onion, chopped
- 3 garlic cloves, minced
- 4 cups vegetable or chicken broth
- 1 cup cream (optional)
- Salt and pepper to taste
- Fresh parsley, chopped (for garnish)

**Instructions:**

1. Heat olive oil in a large pot over medium heat. Sauté onion, garlic, and leeks until softened.
2. Add diced potatoes and broth. Bring to a boil, then reduce heat and simmer for 20-25 minutes until potatoes are tender.
3. Use an immersion blender or transfer to a blender to puree the soup until smooth.
4. Stir in cream (if using) and season with salt and pepper.
5. Serve hot, garnished with fresh parsley.

# Slow-Cooker Beef Ragu

**Ingredients:**

- 2 lbs beef chuck roast
- 2 tbsp olive oil
- 1 onion, chopped
- 2 garlic cloves, minced
- 1 can crushed tomatoes
- 1 cup red wine (optional)
- 1 tsp dried oregano
- 1 tsp dried basil
- Salt and pepper to taste
- Fresh parsley, chopped (for garnish)

**Instructions:**

1. Heat olive oil in a skillet over medium-high heat and brown the beef roast on all sides. Transfer to a slow cooker.
2. In the same skillet, sauté onion and garlic until softened, then add to the slow cooker.
3. Add crushed tomatoes, red wine, oregano, basil, salt, and pepper to the slow cooker. Stir to combine.
4. Cover and cook on low for 6-8 hours or until the beef is tender and can be shredded easily with a fork.
5. Shred the beef and stir it into the sauce. Serve over pasta or polenta, garnished with fresh parsley.

## Baked Ziti with Meatballs

**Ingredients:**

- 1 lb ziti pasta
- 2 cups marinara sauce
- 1 lb ground beef
- 1/2 cup breadcrumbs
- 1 egg
- 1/4 cup Parmesan cheese
- 2 cups mozzarella cheese, shredded
- Salt and pepper to taste
- Fresh basil, chopped (for garnish)

**Instructions:**

1. Cook ziti according to package instructions and set aside.
2. Preheat the oven to 375°F (190°C).
3. In a bowl, mix ground beef, breadcrumbs, egg, Parmesan cheese, salt, and pepper. Form into small meatballs.
4. Brown meatballs in a skillet over medium heat until cooked through, then set aside.
5. In a baking dish, layer marinara sauce, cooked pasta, meatballs, and mozzarella cheese.
6. Bake for 20-25 minutes, or until the cheese is bubbly and golden.
7. Garnish with fresh basil and serve.

## Chicken Cacciatore

**Ingredients:**

- 4 chicken thighs, bone-in and skin-on
- 2 tbsp olive oil
- 1 onion, chopped
- 2 bell peppers, sliced
- 1 can diced tomatoes
- 1 cup dry white wine
- 1 tsp dried oregano
- 1 tsp dried basil
- 1/2 tsp red pepper flakes
- Salt and pepper to taste
- Fresh parsley, chopped (for garnish)

**Instructions:**

1. Heat olive oil in a large skillet over medium-high heat. Brown the chicken thighs on both sides, then set aside.
2. In the same skillet, sauté onion and bell peppers until softened.
3. Add diced tomatoes, white wine, oregano, basil, red pepper flakes, salt, and pepper. Stir to combine.
4. Return chicken to the skillet, skin-side up, and simmer for 30-40 minutes until the chicken is cooked through and tender.
5. Garnish with fresh parsley and serve with pasta or rice.

**Beef and Sweet Potato Stew**

**Ingredients:**

- 1 lb beef stew meat
- 2 tbsp olive oil
- 1 onion, chopped
- 3 garlic cloves, minced
- 2 sweet potatoes, peeled and diced
- 3 carrots, sliced
- 4 cups beef broth
- 1 tsp thyme
- Salt and pepper to taste

**Instructions:**

1. Heat olive oil in a large pot over medium heat. Brown the beef stew meat, then remove and set aside.
2. In the same pot, sauté onion and garlic until softened.
3. Add sweet potatoes, carrots, beef broth, thyme, salt, and pepper. Bring to a boil, then reduce heat and simmer for 1-1.5 hours until the beef is tender.
4. Serve hot with crusty bread.

# Spinach and Ricotta Stuffed Shells

**Ingredients:**

- 1 lb jumbo pasta shells
- 2 cups ricotta cheese
- 1 cup spinach, chopped
- 1 egg
- 1 cup mozzarella cheese, shredded
- 2 cups marinara sauce
- 1/4 cup Parmesan cheese, grated
- Salt and pepper to taste

**Instructions:**

1. Cook pasta shells according to package instructions and set aside.
2. Preheat the oven to 375°F (190°C).
3. In a bowl, mix ricotta cheese, spinach, egg, mozzarella, salt, and pepper.
4. Stuff each shell with the ricotta mixture and place in a baking dish.
5. Pour marinara sauce over the stuffed shells and top with Parmesan cheese.
6. Bake for 20-25 minutes, or until bubbly and golden. Serve hot.

## Vegetarian Chili with Quinoa

**Ingredients:**

- 1 cup quinoa
- 1 can black beans, drained and rinsed
- 1 can kidney beans, drained and rinsed
- 1 can diced tomatoes
- 1 onion, chopped
- 2 garlic cloves, minced
- 1 bell pepper, chopped
- 1 zucchini, chopped
- 1 tsp cumin
- 1 tsp chili powder
- 1/2 tsp paprika
- Salt and pepper to taste

**Instructions:**

1. Cook quinoa according to package instructions and set aside.
2. In a large pot, sauté onion, garlic, bell pepper, and zucchini until softened.
3. Add beans, diced tomatoes, cumin, chili powder, paprika, salt, and pepper. Bring to a boil, then reduce to a simmer for 20-30 minutes.
4. Stir in cooked quinoa and cook for an additional 5 minutes.
5. Serve hot with toppings such as sour cream, cheese, or cilantro.

## Sausage and Potato Bake

**Ingredients:**

- 4 sausages (your choice of variety)
- 4 large potatoes, peeled and cut into cubes
- 2 tbsp olive oil
- 1 onion, chopped
- 2 garlic cloves, minced
- 1 tsp dried thyme
- 1 tsp paprika
- Salt and pepper to taste
- Fresh parsley, chopped (for garnish)

**Instructions:**

1. Preheat the oven to 400°F (200°C).
2. Heat olive oil in a skillet over medium heat. Brown the sausages on all sides, then remove from the skillet and set aside.
3. In the same skillet, sauté onion and garlic until softened.
4. In a baking dish, layer the cubed potatoes, cooked onion and garlic, sausage, thyme, paprika, salt, and pepper.
5. Roast in the oven for 30-40 minutes, or until the potatoes are tender and the sausages are cooked through, turning halfway through.
6. Garnish with fresh parsley and serve hot.

## Braised Lamb Shanks with Mashed Potatoes

**Ingredients:**

- 2 lamb shanks
- 2 tbsp olive oil
- 1 onion, chopped
- 2 garlic cloves, minced
- 2 cups beef broth
- 1 cup red wine
- 1 tsp rosemary
- Salt and pepper to taste
- 4 large potatoes, peeled and cut into chunks
- 1/4 cup butter
- 1/2 cup milk

**Instructions:**

1. Preheat the oven to 325°F (165°C).
2. Heat olive oil in a large oven-safe pot over medium-high heat. Brown the lamb shanks on all sides and set them aside.
3. In the same pot, sauté onion and garlic until softened. Add beef broth, red wine, rosemary, salt, and pepper.
4. Return the lamb shanks to the pot, cover, and braise in the oven for 2.5-3 hours, or until the meat is tender and falling off the bone.
5. Meanwhile, cook the potatoes in a pot of boiling salted water until tender, about 15 minutes. Drain and mash with butter and milk.
6. Serve the lamb shanks over mashed potatoes, spooning the braising liquid over the top.

## Baked Sweet Potatoes with Sausage and Kale

**Ingredients:**

- 4 large sweet potatoes
- 4 sausages (your choice of variety)
- 1 bunch kale, chopped
- 1 onion, chopped
- 2 garlic cloves, minced
- 2 tbsp olive oil
- Salt and pepper to taste
- 1/2 cup shredded cheese (optional)

**Instructions:**

1. Preheat the oven to 400°F (200°C).
2. Prick the sweet potatoes with a fork and bake them on a baking sheet for 40-50 minutes, or until soft.
3. While the sweet potatoes bake, heat olive oil in a large skillet over medium heat. Brown the sausages, then remove and set aside. Slice the sausages into bite-sized pieces.
4. In the same skillet, sauté onion and garlic until softened. Add kale and cook until wilted.
5. When the sweet potatoes are done, slice them open and fluff the insides with a fork. Top with sausage and kale mixture.
6. Sprinkle with cheese if desired, and serve hot.

**Squash and Bean Chili**

**Ingredients:**

- 1 medium butternut squash, peeled and cubed
- 1 can black beans, drained and rinsed
- 1 can kidney beans, drained and rinsed
- 1 can diced tomatoes
- 1 onion, chopped
- 2 garlic cloves, minced
- 1 bell pepper, chopped
- 1 tsp cumin
- 1 tsp chili powder
- 1/2 tsp paprika
- Salt and pepper to taste
- 4 cups vegetable broth

**Instructions:**

1. In a large pot, sauté onion, garlic, and bell pepper until softened.
2. Add cubed butternut squash, black beans, kidney beans, diced tomatoes, cumin, chili powder, paprika, salt, and pepper.
3. Pour in vegetable broth and bring to a boil. Reduce the heat and simmer for 30-40 minutes, or until the squash is tender.
4. Serve hot, optionally garnished with sour cream or cheese.

# Fish and Chips

**Ingredients:**

- 4 white fish fillets (such as cod or haddock)
- 2 large russet potatoes, peeled and cut into fries
- 1 cup all-purpose flour
- 1 tsp baking powder
- 1/2 tsp salt
- 1 cup cold sparkling water
- Vegetable oil for frying
- Lemon wedges (for serving)

**Instructions:**

1. Preheat the oven to 425°F (220°C). Place the potato fries on a baking sheet, drizzle with olive oil, and bake for 25-30 minutes, flipping halfway, until golden and crispy.
2. While the fries bake, prepare the batter for the fish. In a bowl, whisk together flour, baking powder, and salt. Slowly add cold sparkling water to form a smooth batter.
3. Heat vegetable oil in a deep pan or fryer to 350°F (175°C).
4. Dip the fish fillets into the batter, then fry for 4-5 minutes until golden and crispy.
5. Serve the fish with the baked chips and lemon wedges.

## Sweet and Sour Pork

**Ingredients:**

- 1 lb pork tenderloin, cut into bite-sized pieces
- 1 onion, chopped
- 1 bell pepper, chopped
- 1/2 cup pineapple chunks
- 1/4 cup soy sauce
- 1/4 cup rice vinegar
- 3 tbsp sugar
- 2 tbsp ketchup
- 1 tsp cornstarch mixed with 2 tbsp water
- Salt and pepper to taste
- 2 tbsp vegetable oil

**Instructions:**

1. Heat vegetable oil in a large skillet over medium-high heat. Cook the pork pieces until browned on all sides, then remove and set aside.
2. In the same skillet, sauté onion and bell pepper until softened. Add pineapple chunks.
3. In a small bowl, whisk together soy sauce, rice vinegar, sugar, and ketchup. Pour over the vegetables in the skillet.
4. Return the pork to the skillet and stir in the cornstarch mixture. Cook for 2-3 minutes until the sauce thickens.
5. Serve hot with rice.

## Stuffed Acorn Squash with Quinoa

**Ingredients:**

- 2 acorn squash, halved and seeded
- 1 cup quinoa
- 1/4 cup dried cranberries
- 1/4 cup chopped nuts (such as pecans or walnuts)
- 1 onion, chopped
- 2 garlic cloves, minced
- 2 tbsp olive oil
- 1 tsp cinnamon
- Salt and pepper to taste

**Instructions:**

1. Preheat the oven to 375°F (190°C).
2. Place the acorn squash halves on a baking sheet, drizzle with olive oil, and roast for 30-40 minutes, or until tender.
3. Meanwhile, cook the quinoa according to package instructions.
4. In a skillet, heat olive oil and sauté onion and garlic until softened. Stir in cinnamon, salt, and pepper.
5. In a bowl, combine cooked quinoa, sautéed onion and garlic, dried cranberries, and chopped nuts.
6. Spoon the quinoa mixture into the roasted acorn squash halves and serve hot.

www.ingramcontent.com/pod-product-compliance
Lightning Source LLC
LaVergne TN
LVHW081338060526
838201LV00055B/2730